Pro-Life in Action

Fr Andrzej Muszala

*All booklets are published
thanks to the generosity of the supporters
of the Catholic Truth Society*

All rights reserved. First published 2021 by The Incorporated Catholic Truth Society, 42-46 Harleyford Road, London SE11 5AY. Tel: 020 7640 0042. © 2021 Fr Andrzej Muszala. www.ctsbooks.org

ISBN 978 1 78469 660 3

Contents

Introduction 7

Part One: Forgetting about yourself – forming a proper relationship with others, with the world and with yourself 11
    Jesus Christ – the source of prayer in action 12
    Thinking about others 17
    Being ready to serve 22
    A proper relationship with one another within the family 29
    Love for nature 36
    Forming a proper relationship with yourself 40

Part Two: Trust – the correct relationship with God 53
    The beauty of silent prayer 54
    God is present in every event 56
    …when we suffer, in sickness and when we die 59
    God approaches us in every person we meet 62
    Life in the presence of God 66
    Living every minute 70
    Constant prayer 74
    The end 78

*We either pray constantly
or we don't pray at all.*

W. Stinissen

Dear Reader

This is the second in a series of publications on silent prayer. Together they form an introduction to prayer in the spirit of Jesus. Our Lord, who was constantly alert to the gentle whispers of the Holy Spirit, established a new way of life based on constant prayer – "prayer in action". Let us look at this in greater depth.

Fr Andrzej Muszala

INTRODUCTION

When the time you have put aside for prayer has come to an end, what then? We all know that prayer should never finish. "Always be joyful, pray constantly," wrote St Paul to the Thessalonians (*1 Th* 5:17). Jesus told us that prayer should never cease (*Lk* 18:1). This has often been misinterpreted as the requirement to practise the mental repetition of devotional utterances such as verses from the Bible. Yet, how is it possible to do this? Can a surgeon focus on prayer while maintaining total concentration as he carries out a complicated operation? What about a student who has to prepare a dissertation, perform experiments in a lab or learn a new language? Surely the supermarket cashier dealing with customers all day at the checkout cannot be thinking of anything else. Wouldn't these people be in danger of performing their work negligently if they were constantly preoccupied with repeating words of prayer?

That is not the way Jesus behaved nor does he ask us to do two things at the same time. True understanding of constant prayer comes only when we grasp what prayer actually is. If we regard prayer as a conversation with God, the danger is that we will concentrate on using words. We will end up talking all the time! If, as the saints did, we understand the true meaning of prayer, we will be on the right lines. St Thérèse of Lisieux tells us: "For me, prayer is an uplifting of the heart, a glance towards heaven, a cry of gratitude and love, uttered equally in sorrow and in joy. In a word it is something noble, supernatural, which expands my soul and unites it to God" (St Thérèse of Lisieux, *Manuscript C*, 25r-v).

A *conversation* with God is not mentioned at all in St Thérèse's description of prayer. Her definition reveals something more important. Prayer is an uplifting of the heart – an act of love. When we love someone, we do so all the time and we constantly show our love by deeds rather than words. Love is communicated at the level of the heart: *cor ad cor loquitur* – heart speaks to heart (St John Henry Newman).

Prayer is a glance towards heaven, and heaven is mirrored in other people, in the beauty of the world, at the base of the soul and everywhere that God exists.

Prayer is a cry of gratitude and love – an act of love performed in the midst of our work, regardless of whether we are happy, relaxed or exhausted.

Prayer is something noble and supernatural. Through prayer we are transported into another realm and we are united with the Holy Spirit. The everyday things we do become extraordinary – the surgeon operating on a patient becomes more focused and precise; the student works more efficiently and with greater attention to detail; for the cashier in a shop, work is no longer a boring routine but it is an opportunity to show helpfulness and warmth in serving customers.

God remains in constant dialogue with us. He "speaks" to us all the time through the various events and the people we encounter throughout the day. Our job is to be vigilant at all times and to react accordingly. This is the essence of "prayer in action".

Prayer in action is the continuation of silent prayer once we have left the "room" in our heart. Prayer in action is just as intense as prayer in silence but in a different way. What links these two modes of prayer is the fact that we are giving ourselves entirely to others, as God does: the Greatest Love.

According to St Thérèse of Lisieux, the definition of love is "to give away everything and give yourself entirely". This is to invest one talent in order to gain ten.

The first five talents are gained as we make the daily ascent during silent prayer – completely forgetful of ourselves: 5 x NOTHING.

The next five talents are gained by our prayer in action when we are prepared to serve and give our lives entirely, keeping nothing for ourselves: 5 x EVERYTHING.

- **The First Everything**: *the Foundation, Jesus Christ.*
- **The Second Everything**: *achieving a proper relationship with others.*
- **The Third Everything**: *achieving a proper relationship with the world.*
- **The Fourth Everything**: *achieving a proper relationship with myself.* I must remember to FORGET ABOUT MYSELF just as Jesus did: "He did not count equality with God something to be grasped. But he emptied himself, taking the form of a slave" (*Ph* 2:6-7).
- **The Fifth Everything**: *achieving a proper relationship with God.* To do this we must have total TRUST in God, just as Jesus showed us by his example: "Thy will be done".

Let us now analyse these in detail.

PART ONE:

FORGETTING ABOUT YOURSELF – FORMING A PROPER RELATIONSHIP WITH OTHERS, WITH THE WORLD AND WITH YOURSELF

*Unless a wheat grain falls on the ground
and dies, it remains only a single grain;
but if it dies, it yields a rich harvest.*

(Jn 12:24)

Jesus Christ – the source of prayer in action

Jesus is offering himself on the altar to God. In his constant offering he finds everyday bread for himself.

(Fr Marie-Eugène, *I Want to See God*)

If constant prayer provides the ground our love for God springs from, then prayer in action has the same function: it enables us to give everything to God who has conquered our hearts with the arrow of his tender love. In silent prayer we seek Jesus inside ourselves, deep within our souls, whereas, by prayer in action, we seek him externally, in the people and events that we encounter. It would be impossible to describe all the possible situations we are likely to meet: we can only offer a few scenarios and show how they might be examples for us in our daily lives.

What a challenge this is! We each have our own daily agenda. We are all hermits in a way; solitary when it comes to reflecting, making decisions, making more and more demands of ourselves and, basically, trying to be a balanced individual. In a nutshell, we have to develop the art of living our own life, not just slavishly following others. It is not a matter of just copying the life of Jesus or the saints. It is about asking ourselves how we might change our life into a great act of love by observing their example of giving themselves to serve others. We can then find how we can do the same in our own daily activities.

A question comes to mind: why should we do this? Why should we spend our lives serving others and forgetting about ourselves? After all, many present-day trends are concerned with self-motivation, assertiveness and taking care of our own business. The answer is inscribed on the very first page of the Bible – we were created in God's own image (*Gn* 1:27). He is Love itself. He is Love that is constantly being given away. He lives for others, he thinks about others and he seeks the happiness of others.

Adam respected the law of nature. He took care of plants and animals. He gave away the part of his body nearest his heart for God to create a woman: "Bone of my bones, and flesh of my flesh! She is to be called woman, because she was taken from man" (*Gn* 2:23).

The more he gave away the happier he was until the moment when he reached for the fruit of the tree of good and evil.

By picking the forbidden fruit, Man did something against his primal nature. This was a selfish deed. Consumerism, greed, competitiveness, the urge to be like God – to play God – that is the essence of the Fall of the first man. A poisonous selfishness was brought into the world; the struggle to achieve our own desires displaced the act of serving others; instead of forgetting about ourselves so that others might be served, we preferred to concentrate on our personal ambitions, to indulge our desires and gratify bodily lust. Love was replaced by self-indulgence. Man lost the ability to understand himself. He became selfish and departed from God. "From then onwards man lives on earth with all the virtues confused; he lives on earth where values no longer make sense" (J.C. Lachert, *Therapy for the Spiritual Illness*).

However God, being our Father, couldn't just leave us like that. He wanted to save his children and restore the primal harmony. "When the appointed time came, God sent his Son, born of a woman, born a subject to the Law, to redeem the subjects of the Law and to enable us to be adopted as sons" (*Ga* 4:4).

At a particular moment in time someone extraordinary came into this world. True God and truly human, he became known later as Jesus of Nazareth. From the very first moment he communicated by what he did rather than solely by the words he spoke. He lived for his Father and for other people, never for himself.

When he prayed, he always turned to God the Father. "Hallowed be thy name. Thy kingdom come, thy will, not mine, be done". In serving his brothers and sisters he healed, uplifted and taught them. He saved the prostitute, he multiplied the loaves of bread, he changed water into wine and he raised Lazarus from death. He took notice of the needs of others; he served them and spent himself, even to the last drop of his blood, on the cross, allowing his heart to be pierced and retaining nothing for himself. Jesus himself was the gift.

With regard to the world as it is now, God is saying to us, "It was not like that at the very beginning. Then there was no ego in the world, only pure love. Minds were not narrowly focused on selfish gain but were open to the needs of others."

We must go back to this prototype, and this we can do by simply looking at Jesus in the same way as Mary did when she chose to sit at his feet and listen.

This is the first EVERYTHING which is the basis for prayer in action. "If anyone wants to be a follower of mine, let him renounce himself and take up his cross every day and follow me" (*Lk* 9:23).

The streams of our desire need to return to the Source, which is the Holy Spirit. This is very difficult. This is like asking the current of the river to flow upstream. "If you want to find the source, you have to go up, against the current, tear through, seek, don't give up" (John Paul II, *Roman Triptych*).

The second EVERYTHING is achieved by our attitude towards other people, by the way we regard their well-being, by the way we look after them and by the way we relate to the members of our families.

Thinking about others

The best way to stop thinking about yourself is to think about others.

(W. Stinissen, *Deep Calls to Deep*)

We are used to thinking primarily about ourselves. We do it automatically since our thoughts and reactions are governed by our feelings and emotions and, as a result, we tend to be preoccupied by personal matters. Do we ever pause for a while to think over some issue that does not arise immediately from our own concerns?

Unfortunately, because we are distracted by the world of commerce, the media, the internet and other people, not to mention our own desires, we allow life to pass us by without reflecting on how we are being manipulated. We tend to live for this immediate moment without ever considering where it is all leading. We lack the ability to discipline our thinking. Maybe we have never thought deeply about things throughout our whole life. Today is the day we should wake up! St Paul urges us: "Wake up from your sleep, rise from the dead, and Christ will shine on you. So be very careful about the sort of lives you lead, like intelligent and not like senseless people. This may be a wicked age, but your lives should redeem it" (*Ep* 5:14-17).

It is a very hard work to reflect. It is harder than building a house, gardening, cleaning, doing the washing up, cooking or digging a ditch. No wonder people tend to escape from reflection to do other things that free them from thinking. No wonder that we tend to find anything that we can use as an excuse to avoid sitting down and spending time in quiet contemplation and spiritual reading.

Thinking is what allows us to realise that each of us is an individual person whom God has created, and it enables us to be conscious of our unique identity and destiny.

"I think therefore I am," said the philosopher Descartes. Make the effort to think! Don't escape! Short moments of reflection will lead you to finding yourself and to a spiritual uplifting.

However, just "thinking" is not enough. We must think about others and consider their happiness rather than our own. The prayer that Jesus began in the desert continued into his healing ministry as his attention was drawn to God's presence in those he met.

Thinking about others means seeing them as children of God and each as a temple of the Holy Spirit. This is especially important when we meet a child of God who, perhaps, is struggling with addiction, is violent or aggressive, is simply irritating or is just someone we see regularly yet fail to notice. "Be awake!" says Jesus.

Thinking about others means being vigilant; staying alert to notice if there is somebody nearby with problems or disabilities. What is the good of going to church if I have left my car in the disabled bay, obstructed emergency exit doors or blocked somebody else's car in? How should I expect God to listen to me if I am muttering my prayers out loud, disturbing those who have come to pray in silence? How caring am I if I am taking up extra space in a pew and depriving someone of a seat, someone who may then be forced to stand? Am I one of those passengers on the train, chatting loudly on my mobile phone, disturbing other passengers who wish to sit in quiet and work or read their book?

Lack of awareness of others can be seen in many ways. There are many examples of lack of respect for others. Noisy and intrusive behaviour such as piercing laughter, rowdy shouting in the streets, playing loud music in a block of flats or in restaurants is common. Forceful and bullying behaviour on the roads, being wasteful with food, fly-tipping rubbish in rural areas or in neighbourhood streets are other illustrations of an uncaring attitude. Over the years society has created a behavioural code known as courtesy or good manners in order to show how to give respect to others. This is reflected in behaviour such as permitting an elderly person to go first through a door or offering a seat on a crowded bus; acknowledging neighbours or greeting passers-by on a country walk; refraining from causing intrusive noise at antisocial times; respecting non-smoking areas; observing the politeness of saying "please", "thank you" and "sorry". We could make an endless list. These are small gestures but they are more pleasing to God than the praying of rosaries because they are harder actions to perform. Do we really pay enough attention to how we behave?

When we show concern for our fellow human beings, we should act in a way that helps them to grow. We have the example of Jesus who taught, explained, repeated and listened to the disciples and the crowds. He spoke patiently to individuals such as the Samaritan woman, Nicodemus and the blind man. On occasion he even reprimanded Peter, James and John.

"If your brother does something wrong, go and have it out with him alone, between your two selves. If he listens to you, you have won back your brother" (*Mt* 18:15). Jesus was gentle, but if this didn't bring the desired result he was not afraid to raise his voice and reprimand: "Get behind me, Satan! You are an obstacle in my path, because the way you think is not God's way but man's" (*Mt* 17:23). And also: "Alas for you, scribes and Pharisees, you hypocrites! You who shut up the kingdom of heaven in man's faces, neither going in yourselves nor allowing others to go in who want to" (*Mt* 23:13). This apparent harshness in the way Jesus reacted did not mean he was angry, but that he chose to use a radical method of impressing someone who displayed hardness of heart.

In order to save them he was prepared to risk falling out of favour with them. Harsh words were always addressed to scribes and Pharisees while, towards other sinners, he showed gentle compassion, offering help and, in some cases, preserving them from death by stoning. He was a good shepherd.

Caring for others does not mean we should do everything for them. They should do their own work in order to grow and develop. If you see someone struggling with a task, you may be torn between taking over and allowing the person to find the solution unaided. This requires a decision. Each case is different and there is no set pattern as to how we should or should not intervene. How hard it is to think about others! But this is what allows us to forget about ourselves, and this is the essence of spiritual life. Therefore thinking about others is a prayer. Constant prayer.

Being ready to serve

My main task is now trying to forget about myself. One doesn't lose anything by doing this as he finds Jesus in everybody and one can serve everybody more.

(Fr Marie-Eugène, letter to a friend, 6th May 1922)

There is a pattern to serving one another which was established by Jesus in the last days of his life when he did three particular things: washed his disciples' feet, established the Eucharist, and died on the Cross.

When Jesus washed the disciples' feet he said:

> Do you understand," he said, "what I have done to you? You call me Master and Lord, and rightly; so I am. If I, then, the Lord and Master, have washed your feet, you should wash each other's feet. I have given you an example so that you may copy what I have done to you. I tell you most solemnly, no servant is greater than his master, no messenger is greater than the man who sent him. Now that you know this, happiness will be yours if you behave accordingly. (*Jn* 13:12-17)

In ancient times, a slave would have a bowl of water ready for when his master returned from the *agora* (the marketplace, or public assembly). As soon as his master arrived, the slave would remove his sandals and wash the dirt from his feet. Because it was the action of a slave, when Peter saw that Jesus was doing the same for the disciples, he shouted, "Never! You shall never wash my feet!" But Jesus said, "Do this to others as I have done it for you." In other words, he was saying that we shall be blessed by doing simple things to show our love for one another.

Jesus was asking us to do simple, everyday things but to do them with great love. There are many examples of occasions when we can do this. At a simple level we can pass the bread at meal times, we can offer water to a hot and thirsty person and we can show friendship by accepting invitations to parties when we would prefer to be elsewhere. More significantly, there are opportunities to visit the sick – in hospital or at home, to visit prisoners, to give shelter to a refugee, to donate clothing to the poor and groceries to a food bank. We can also be alert to the needs of the community around us, especially to those who are distressed, hurt, lonely or bereaved. Such deeds of kindness are similar to the "widow's mite" – a small contribution that may seem trivial in the eyes of the world but is priceless in the eyes of God.

There are patterns of behaviour that typify a prayerful person.

A kind and polite shopkeeper is helpful to customers in a shop. Instead of chatting to her colleague and, despite her tiredness, she helps the customer to choose, answering their queries with patience and courtesy. In so doing, within a couple of minutes, she has demonstrated multiple acts of love for others. She is not even aware she is doing something as beautiful and worthy as praying the Rosary.

A student, living on the sixth floor, always seems to have a smile for her neighbours while standing together in the lift. She is good-natured and always has time for a few friendly words with them. Gradually more people notice her and they begin to wonder who this pleasant and polite student is who happens to live in their block of flats.

A mother of a disabled son takes him shopping, to church and out for walks. She is always watchful that he doesn't hurt himself because of his lack of bodily co-ordination. She patiently explains things to him dozens of times, although some people would tell her it is pointless. She doesn't give up but devotes herself to his care to the best of her ability. This is her personal example of constant prayer.

Patients look forward to the shift of the nurse who is kind and polite to them; a nurse who knows their names and is thorough in caring for them. This nurse speaks clearly, and loudly enough for them to hear and understand. The nurse who gets to know the personal situation of each patient brings a little sunshine and warmth into their grey world of suffering, and is a more effective carer than one who is indifferent to their individual needs.

A classroom teacher is on the lookout for those children who are disadvantaged, the ones from broken or dysfunctional homes and those who are bullied. This teacher takes care to prepare properly for classes and to ensure that all the pupils are able to understand the lessons. This teacher is devoted to the pupils and tries year upon year to do better for them and is delighted when they do well.

A politician shows respect for counterparts in the opposition party, avoiding offensive language or aggressive tactics. He listens carefully and earnestly tries to help the people he represents. He detests corruption of any kind.

Volunteer, priest, midwife, courier, taxi driver, waiter, nun, cook, accountant, architect, engineer, bishop…each of them can give their life to serve others. Step by step.

"We give priority over ourselves to those we really love" (T. Halik, *I Want You to Be*). Living life in this way makes sense of the notion of taking the Eucharist to others. Your days are turned into constant liturgy where you and angels sing, "Holy, Holy, Holy Lord". You are giving yourself to others: just like Jesus did. "Take this bread and eat it; this is my body… Take this cup and drink from it; this is my blood…" The body symbolises the material things that we have been given so that we can be of service. In this way we are equipped to serve, just like the Samaritan who spared time for the wounded traveller and gave him two denarii and a donkey, or like Zacchaeus who gave away half of his possessions.

"Give, and there will be gifts for you; a full measure, pressed down, shaken together, and running over, will be poured into your lap; because the amount you measure out is the amount you will be given back" (*Lk* 6:38). The more you give the happier you are, and whatever you give will multiply. "Our body was given to us for us to give it away. Our body needs to be 'given away'" (W. Stinissen, *The Bread We Eat*).

The ancient Israelites thought blood was the bearer of the soul. As blood circulates throughout the whole body it gives oxygen to all the cells and in a mysterious way transmits life itself. Therefore, giving blood was seen as endowing someone with spiritual values such as kindness, patience, hope, happiness, strength, faith and justice. All these values have their source in our soul and, nourished by the sacrament of the Holy Eucharist, we can be bread and wine for others, both in a practical and a spiritual manner.

"A person works not in order to feed himself but his relatives. We were created in order to serve others and not to serve and live for ourselves" (W. Stinissen, *The Bread*

We Eat). The greatest act of love is to give one's life for another. After washing his disciples' feet and breaking the bread and drinking the wine, Jesus died on the cross. His last words were: "Father, into your hands I commit my spirit" (*Lk* 23:46). We are dying every minute. As we get older our bodies' cells degenerate. People nowadays are desperately anxious to prevent this process; they spend fortunes on plastic surgery without achieving anything as a result. They are not aware that there is no greater love than to give your life for others. That is the biggest PARADOX of the Bible.

In order to gain EVERYTHING, we are required to give away everything. In order to gain happiness, we need to stop searching for it. In order to live our lives to the full, we must die.

Once we can come to understand this, and to see that, above all else, we want to give of ourselves so that others may have life, then we would not hesitate to donate a kidney, to jump into the water to help a drowning person or to carry on with a pregnancy despite there being a risk. We would begin to see that death is the greatest and final act of love and the ultimate fulfilment of happiness. After a while, we would be able to see that death is nothing to fear but we would be able to embrace death as our sister who will lead us to the Beloved.

> Set me like a seal on your heart,
> Like a seal on your arm.
> For life is strong as Death,
> Jealously relentless as Sheol.
> The flash of it is a flash of fire,
> a flame of the Lord himself.
> Love no flood can quench,
> No torrents drown. (*Sg* 8:6)

Your life will burn down like a candle at the altar. All will be done as you pray the priestly prayer of Christ in silence:

> Father, glorify your Son so that your Son may glorify you; and, through the power over all mankind that you have given him, let him give eternal life to all those you have entrusted to him… I have made your name known to the men you took from the world to give me. They were yours and you gave them to me, and they have kept your word… I pray for them; I am not praying for the world but for those you have given me, because they belong to you… With me in them and you in me, may they be so completely one that the world will realise that it was you who sent me and that I have loved them as much as you loved me… I am not asking you to remove them from the world, but to protect them from the evil one. Consecrate them in the truth; your word is truth… And for their sake I consecrate myself so that they too may be consecrated in truth. (*Jn* 17)

A proper relationship with one another within the family

How do we maintain good relationships within our family? This can be complicated because we have close blood ties; we are emotionally bonded and, frequently, we share the same household.

Jesus had his own family too. He was brought up to be an independent young man and learnt to make his own choices. He also helped his parents to recognise their own identity. His upbringing wasn't all rosy. There were times he stood up to his mother saying: "Why were you looking for me? Did you not know that I must be busy with my Father's affairs?" (*Lk* 2:49). Harsh words…but this was Love speaking.

Years later, when Mary stood at the foot of the cross, she remembered what Jesus had said. She realised that his words were needed in order to prepare her for the way of the cross and the death of her son, when her suffering would prove to be much greater.

The relationship between an engaged couple

Being in love and being engaged is an intense time when a new family is being formed. It is a time of extraordinary feelings and attractions.

This is the time when a young man and a young woman should "switch on" their brain, even though it is difficult to do so while the heart is being propelled towards the loved one. Nevertheless, it is important to step back and consider the whole situation. Will we make each other happy? Do we share the same values of faith and of serving others? Do we both wish to pursue the habits of contemplation, prayer and living a spiritual life? Do we have the same approach to bringing up children? Are we looking beyond physical attraction and desire? Is there any pressure from the "biological clock"? Might there be an extraordinary age gap? Furthermore, might there be an objective impediment to the marriage such as a former marriage or priestly vows?

Don't be afraid to ask a friend for an impartial opinion. There may be factors that you have failed to take into consideration. Remember that being in love blinds the ability to think straight. By acting impulsively, following only your feelings, you may well be disappointed by unforeseen consequences. True love is built on more than physical and emotional desires and requires a mutual harmony at all levels. Making a good life choice is definitely not easy. It is even more difficult to step back when your heart is bleeding with love…

To abandon a relationship that you know would be a grave mistake will hurt dreadfully, but trust that God has something even more beautiful for you. Something greater is waiting for you.

The relationship between a married couple

If you are married, don't revisit your past. You are with the person whom God has given to you: the one with whom you will grow in mutual participation.

The most important thing in marriage is equality. There should be no domination from either partner. It is very often the case that those who assume a dominant role in marriage cannot recognise this in their own behaviour, and it is almost impossible to get them to acknowledge that they are behaving in this way. What's more, they are convinced that they are the ones who are constantly being upset. They don't realise that it is their own ego demanding that everything conforms to their will.

The love between married couples has four stages:

Stage 1 "I have fallen in love with you"
This means: I love myself more than I love you. I cannot live without you. As time passes, I am becoming jealous and start to control and check whether you are spending more time with others than with me. How unfortunate for those whose relationship fails to develop from this stage as their life as a couple will become a nightmare and will turn into hell!

Stage 2 "I love you"
This means: I am placing your happiness before my own. I want you to grow and to know that I will always be at your side to support you. I will never let you down.

Stage 3 "I love you and our children"

The act of love bears fruit in the form of our children. If for some reason this does not happen, we must not distort nature in pursuit of having children at all costs. For example, in vitro fertilisation leads to many "extra" embryos being frozen, and surrogacy treats both the birth mother and child as a commodity rather than a person, but there are other ways of becoming parents, even if a couple cannot have their own children. Many children are in need of adoptive or foster parents, and those who care for these children are truly parents. By adopting them we can embrace and love them just like children from our own flesh and blood: "Anyone who welcomes a little child like this in my name welcomes me" (*Mt* 18:5).

If every married couple who cannot have children of their own were to adopt two orphans, there would be no orphans left in the world.

Alternatively, a couple could satisfy their parental role by providing an ongoing supply of material and spiritual support for children in need.

Stage 4 "I love you and our children and our love goes out to others"

This is the fullness of love extending beyond our family and going out to the streets, hospitals, hospices and orphanages. We see each other's needs rather than our own. Marriage does not cause us to abandon our spiritual ambitions. On the contrary, marriage should urge us to make them become reality.

The act of love between a married couple is an ecstasy in which each loses him- or herself for the other and in which each forgets about him- or herself. The happiness of the other person is paramount. Together, you show each other kindness, gentleness and patience; you are good and loving. You become one body and one spirit. Don't ignore this: it is your united prayer. It is the corridor leading to the kingdom of heaven.

Relationships between parents and children

Procreation does not only mean creating new life in the biological sense. It also means carefully bringing up the children. If you love them, devote your time to them, nurture them, take care of their needs, talk to them, teach them how to pray and show them how to live according to proper values, then you are a good parent.

Don't spoil your children. Don't allow them to rule you. Don't buy them everything they want. Don't even engage in discussion about it with a very young child. Children learn more from example than from words. Don't permit a child to do whatever he wants: shouting and running in church, in an aeroplane or in a restaurant; splashing water at the beach; throwing sand at people. Make sure that they give up their seat on a bus to an elderly person who has no seat. Ask your child to help you if you need to and don't do everything for your child if he or she is able to do it by him- or herself. You have a dozen or so years to bring up your child to be a responsible adult. During their early years, children are biddable. If you waste this precious time, don't be surprised if, in later years, you are disappointed by the behaviour of the adult you have brought up.

"Do you have children? Educate them" (*Si* 7:23). Educate your children and don't tie them too much to yourself. They are not your possessions. Allow them to leave home when they grow up and don't resent them for doing so. Think of how Jesus left his mother and went off to fulfil his Father's will. He didn't stop loving her though.

Relationships between children and parents

Are your parents still living? Be thankful for them. Respect them and look after them as they get older. Be kind and patient with them.

> My son, support your father in his old age,
> Do not grieve him during his life.
> Even in his mind should fail, show him sympathy,
> Do not despise him in your health and strength;
> For kindness to a father shall not be forgotten
> But will serve as reparation for your sins. (*Si* 3:12-14)

This doesn't mean that you have to live with your parents or be ready to go running whenever they call. You have to find the right balance between helping your elderly parents and living your own life.

Being single

For some people the opportunity to be married does not present itself. Nevertheless, being unmarried can bring happiness whether or not it is the result of a conscious choice. Being single enables you to develop yourself as a gift for others and for God. Jesus is your beloved one. With him and in him you become everything for everybody.

Widowhood also provides the opportunity to dedicate oneself to the service of God in the same way. In offering one's talents and energy to help others, it is possible to transform one's sense of loss and sorrow into joy and reward, and to move ever closer in unity with Jesus.

In either situation you can pray constantly, fulfilling what God has in mind for you. When you go to bed you can say "Amen". Even as you sleep you are continuing to pray in your complete dedication and trust in Christ.

"I will lie down in peace and sleep comes at once. For you alone, Lord, make me dwell in safety" (*Ps* 4:9).

Love for nature

Since through the grandeur and beauty and the creatures we may, by analogy, contemplate their Author.

(Ws 13:5)

The world is a reflection of the Holy Trinity in its beauty and harmony. Those who practise contemplation can perceive the Lord's presence in the gentle breeze (Elijah), in the powerful sea (St Augustine), in the birds and wolves (St Francis of Assisi), in the mountains and valleys (St John of the Cross), in the thunderstorms and stars (St Thérèse of Lisieux), in meadows (St John Henry Newman) and in lakes and forests (Karol Wojtyła – St John Paul II).

"Look at the birds, look at the lilies", said Jesus. Even the tiniest cell contains the unique beauty of creation. When new life is created "God is celebrating, smiling, giving a fireworks display. New life, new man, new hope and the opportunity to do good deeds" (Ester Chaim).

When you are hiking in the mountains, you are praying. When you go kayaking, you are praising the Lord. When you are resting in a meadow, you are thanking God for this beautiful world. Without words.

As long as you are able to see deeper than just the material surface of things. As long as you can see God in all this beautiful nature of which you are part.

God has written a precious book, "whose letters are the multitude of created things present in the universe". This contemplation of creation allows us to discover, in each thing, a teaching which God wishes to hand on to us, since "for the believer, to contemplate creation is to hear a message, to listen to a paradoxical and silent voice". We can say that, "alongside revelation properly so-called, contained in sacred Scripture, there is a divine manifestation in the blaze of the sun and the fall of night". (Pope Francis, *Laudato Sí*, 85)

In silence we can discover that, within nature, God has given us many rights:

- The right to make a gift of yourself.
  "Any tree that does not produce good fruit is cut down and thrown on the fire" (*Mt* 7:19).

- The right to trust in God.
  "Why, every hair on your head has been counted. So there is no need to be afraid; you are worth more than hundreds of sparrows" (*Mt* 10:30-31).

- The right to develop yourself.
  "Night and day, while he sleeps, when he is awake, the seed is sprouting and growing; how, he does not know" (*Mk* 4:27).

- The right to be united with Christ.
  "I am the vine, you are the branches. Whoever remains

in me, with me in him, bears fruit in plenty; for cut off from me you can do nothing" (*Jn* 15:5).

- The right of passing.
  "As for man, his days are like grass, he flowers like the flower of the field" (*Ps* 102:15).

And many more…

What we should learn from nature is to accept that we need only a minimum to live. This is how Jesus lived in Nazareth, in the desert and among the fields of Galilee. Remember: "Foxes have holes and the birds of the air have nests, but the Son of Man has nowhere to lay his head" (*Mt* 8:20). And: "But as long as we have food and clothing, let us be content with that" (*1 Tm* 6:8).

The point is to be humble in heart and free from attachment to material goods. Then you are truly human. Then you can sing with the whole of nature:

> Praise the Lord from heavens,
> praise him in the heights.
> Praise him, sun and moon,
> praise him, shining stars.
> Praise the Lord from the earth,
> sea creatures and all oceans,
> fire and hail, snow and mist,
> stormy winds that obey his word;
> all mountains and hills,

all fruit trees and cedars,
beasts, wild and tame,
reptiles and birds on the wing.
(…) Let them praise the name of the Lord
for he alone is exalted (…). (*Ps* 148)

"You are just like Adam who was constantly praying in the Garden of Eden" (Dorotheus of Gaza). You are like Noah in his ark. You live in harmony with nature. You take care of it like a good housekeeper. By showing care for nature as a good housekeeper you are pursuing a proper relationship with the whole universe – the third EVERYTHING.

There is a special dimension to your relationship with others in the world of work. The ordered progress achieved through competent and conscientious work enables the development of methodologies to make the earth productive. By your efforts you learn and grow as an individual. You develop a right relationship when you can see your work not merely as a means of making lots of money, but as a path to developing your talents and encouraging others to develop theirs. When you can act humbly as a member of a team and assist any struggling colleagues, you are also demonstrating your willingness to give of yourself. Similarly, when you can refuse the offer of a well-paid job that goes against your moral values, you are showing commitment to a greater good.

Forming a proper relationship with yourself

"If anyone wants to be a follower of mine, let him renounce himself and take up his cross and follow me.

(Mk 8:34)

How do we deal with our ego – the selfishness in us that craves admiration? How can we stop thinking primarily of ourselves? How can I discover the real me that God designed? That is the great challenge that faces us.

In the beginning both mind and body were under the influence of our spirit. Our lives were properly ordered to God and in perfect harmony with God and Nature. Unfortunately, what happened in Eden caused great disruption. When Eve ate the forbidden fruit, we lost the balance of our mind and spirit and became prone to passions. "You are still unspiritual. Isn't that obvious from all the jealousy and wrangling that there is among you, from the way that you go on behaving like ordinary people?" (*1 Co* 3:3).

We have a certain amount of time to rediscover the state of harmony in which our first parents lived. If we start immediately God will be with us. It's worth doing!

The Body

As we stated earlier, the human body, as designed by God, is beautiful and benevolent. Thanks to this gift from God, we are able to communicate, to love one another, to fulfil our dreams and to engender new life. Accordingly, we should endeavour to take care of our health by eating healthy food, taking exercise, maintaining a work-life balance as far as possible within our means. We must remember that our body is a temple of the Holy Spirit and is destined for resurrection. Being a Christian demands respect for the human body. "A man never hates his own body, but he feeds it and looks after it, and that is the way Christ treats the Church" (*Ep* 5:29).

Although we should not despise our body, we must fight against the body's selfishness. That is how we should interpret the words of St Paul when he speaks of making his body obey him: "For me there are no forbidden things; maybe, but not everything does good. I agree there are no forbidden things for me, but I am not going to let anything dominate me. Food is only meant for the stomach, and the stomach for food" (*1 Co* 7:12-13).

It is possible for us to make a habit of a subtle kind of gluttony, constantly snacking while at school, at work, in the street or in front of the TV or computer. How much time do we waste indulging in endless cups of coffee or tea – even during days of retreat or prayer meetings?

Can we really pray or take part in serious conversations while consuming tea and cakes? This can become a bad habit, detrimental to our spiritual life. Jesus showed us example, explaining that there is a time for fasting and a time for feasting.

"The body – this is not meant for fornication; it is for the Lord and the Lord for the body" (*1 Co* 6:13). Sexuality is good, beautiful and essential. Writers often make a comparison between the consummation of the love between husband and wife in the sexual act and the unity between the soul and God in contemplative prayer. Sexual passion has a powerful effect and is capable of completely overwhelming the body and mind. Sadly, sexual activity is frequently engaged in inappropriately, so it is necessary to guard against improper sexual conduct. The common pitfalls are pornography, masturbation, adultery and even more serious and horrifying abuses. Learning to control sexual urges can be a long, arduous journey and may take years. Don't give up! God will appreciate your effort. To him it will be more acceptable than a penitential pilgrimage to a holy shrine: "A little of this pure love is more precious to God and the soul and more beneficial to the Church, even though it seems one is doing nothing, than all these other works put together" (St John of the Cross, *Spiritual Canticle* XXIX, 2). This also applies to personal battles with addictions and substance abuse.

Refraining from using abusive language or from addictive use of the internet and social media can be equated with five pilgrimages to Santiago de Compostela.

Likewise, giving up smoking could be compared to ten pilgrimages, giving up drinking to fifty pilgrimages, while giving up drugs could be seen as worth a hundred pilgrimages. All this takes a tremendous personal effort. What is discouraging is that the addiction can return. It can attack a vulnerable person again. Therefore it is vital to be constantly alert and ready to fight it again and not to slip back, even once. Every day is like a fight with Goliath, but we have to trust God's strength rather than our own.

In some mysterious way God exists in our temptations as in every other part of our lives. He does not tempt us himself, but he allows the temptation to reach us so that we can make the effort to withstand it. "The trials that you have had to bear are no more than people normally have. You can trust God not to let you be tried beyond your strength, and with any trial he will give you a way out of it and the strength to bear it" (*1 Co* 10:13).

If you have thoughts that lead you towards sin or you are drawn to substance abuse, regard this as an immediate alert to make an act of faith; "O Lord, you know everything, you know I love you!" Turn to Mary, Mother of God and to your Patron Saint and ask them for help to turn this trial into a gift of strength to you. This is the real spiritual life. Your suffering becomes a single act of liturgy where you constantly repeat: "O Lord, lead me not into temptation!" Then you are beautifully dressed in the finest clothes, like the beloved.

> You are wholly beautiful, my love,
> And without a blemish.
> You ravish my heart,
> My sister, my promised bride,
> You ravish my heart
> With a single one of your glances,
> With one single pearl of your necklace. (*Sg* 4:7,9)

It is very helpful to find a watchword or prayer to utter when battling with this kind of trial. It can be "Lord, I offer you this battle. Help (this particular person) in his great suffering", or "Take (this person) into your kingdom, or "Unite your Church", or "Let more people unite with you through silent prayer."

Jeanne Marie lived as a hermit for almost forty years in atonement for the slaughter by the Nazis of innocent people in Auschwitz; Thérèse of Lisieux entered the Carmelite Monastery to pray for priests (especially two missionary priests) and to save souls.

If you find a goal for your sacrifice you will find it easier to fight your trials. You will take up the battle knowing it is more powerful than any verbal prayer. Human beings are all interlinked. If you renounce something and offer yourself, somebody else gets a priceless gift from God.

All those who entrust themselves to God in love will bear good fruit (cf. *Jn* 15:5). This fruitfulness is often invisible, elusive and unquantifiable. We can know quite well that our lives will be fruitful, without claiming to know how, or where. Or when. We may be sure that none of our acts of love will be lost, nor any of our acts of sincere concern for others. No single act of love for God will be lost, no generous effort is meaningless, no painful endurance is wasted. All of these encircle our world like a vital force. Sometimes it seems that our work is fruitless, but mission is not like a business transaction or investment, or even a humanitarian activity. It is not a show where we count how many people come as a result of our publicity; it is something much deeper, which escapes all measurement. It may be that the Lord uses our sacrifices to shower blessings in another part of the world which we will never visit. The Holy Spirit works as he wills, when he wills and where he wills; we entrust ourselves without pretending to see striking results. We know only that our commitment is necessary. Let us learn to rest in the tenderness of the arms of the Father amid our creative and generous commitment. Let us keep marching forward; let us give him everything, allowing him to make our efforts bear fruit in his good time.

(Pope Francis, *Evangelii Gaudium*, 279)

Do not forget about the great enemy that comes as years pass by: laziness. It comes in the guise of sluggishness and apathy, conforming to meaningless routine and lacking motivation. Over the years one becomes lazy without noticing. It can destroy everything you've achieved so far. It gives rise to timewasting by watching endless TV programmes, sitting for hours in front of the computer screen or scrolling through your phone.

Feelings

Feelings are necessary for our inner selves to flourish. However, we must be on our guard because feelings can be merely an expression of selfishness. Unless we exercise some restraint, our feelings can run out of control like a bolting horse. Without losing emotional sensitivity, we need to be able to use our intellect to moderate our feelings when they seem to become extreme.

"Love is always patient and kind; it is never jealous, love is never boastful or conceited" (*1 Co* 13:4). This comment of St Paul says it all. Patience heals anger. Anger has been described as "movement against someone who intentionally or by coincidence harmed you" (St Maximus the Greek)[1]. Anger comes in many guises and shows itself in various ways: insulting behaviour, impatience and irritability, intense dislike or hatred and resentful brooding on harm that has been done to us. Anger is a real poison and leads to a sort of "spiritual epilepsy". It makes us blind, paralyses our muscles, harms our brain, harms our soul, and makes us mad (St John Chrysostom). If you react in anger, it is you who have a problem and not the other person. When you find yourself reacting angrily, employ some means of finding patience: close your eyes, bite your tongue, count to ten and think about how much you have unconditionally received from God. Tell him "That's for you. That's my little gift of love for you". And then everything, including your initial angry reaction, will become a prayer.

"Jealousy and anger shorten your days" (*Si* 30:24). Jealousy causes us to look at others as different from ourselves and to resent their success. In some cases (Cain, Hamlet), it leads to tragedy. It was the jealousy of the scribes that led to Jesus's death. Beware of jealousy! Be happy when others are praised or when they succeed. Don't be reluctant to congratulate them. "Neither will I take blighting envy as my travelling companion, for she has nothing in common with Wisdom" (*Ws* 6:23).

---

[1] St Maxim the Greek, *About Ascetic Practice*, 11

And then there is pride. Pride seeks praise and glory. Many renowned authors have warned about the evils of pride and yet it still thrives among us. It infects people in all walks of life. Pride hankers after power and motivates the wielding of that power. Pride covets conspicuous wealth in order to display financial success. Pride craves praise to satisfy the need to show superiority to others. Anybody is liable to fall into the pitfalls of pride. "But, as a man dedicated to God, you must avoid that" (*1 Tm* 6:11).

Beware of praise! Be glad when your efforts have not been appreciated. Accept correction without feeling resentful; regard it as healing medicine given by God the Doctor.

When you attend a function, don't look for the front seats but remain at the back, especially when the most prominent seating offers prestige and displays status. In fact, don't be afraid to refuse such a place if it's offered you.

Avoid talking about yourself. Spend more time listening to what other people have to say and be sensitive to their situation. Hide your efforts. "When you give alms, do not have it trumpeted before you" (*Mt* 6:3). Live your life in truth. Always maintain the truth: even if it gets you into trouble at work, and even if you suffer bullying or lose your job.

If you have done wrong, be brave, own up and apologise. Don't lie to defend yourself. (I wonder what the world would be like if Adam and Eve had only had the courage to approach God and say, "We ate the fruit you told us not to…"). And remember that you are a mere servant. "God refuses the proud and will always favour the humble" (*1 P* 5:5). It is possibly more difficult to allow the Holy Spirit to influence and change our bad habits than it is to climb the highest mountain.

The fourth EVERYTHING really means everything…

Here the words of Jesus become true: "The kingdom of heaven has been subjected to violence and the violent are taking it by storm" (*Mt* 11:12). May you be one of those struggling against violence for, in doing so, you praise the Lord with the most beautiful hymn:

> My heart overflows with noble words.
> To the king I must speak the song I have made;
> My tongue as nimble as the pen of a scribe.
> You are the fairest of the children of men
> And graciousness is poured upon your lips:
> Because God has blessed you for evermore.
> O mighty one, gird your sword upon your thigh;
> In splendour and state, ride on in triumph
> For the cause of truth are goodness and right.
> Take aim with your bow in your dread right hand.
> Your arrows are sharp; peoples fall beneath you.
> The foes of the king fall down and lose heart.
> (*Ps* 44:2-6)

St John of the Cross echoes everything that was written above:

> Strive always to prefer, not that which is easiest,
>   but that which is most difficult;
> Not that which gives most pleasure,
>   but rather that which gives least;
> Not that which is restful,
>   but that which is wearisome;
> Not that which is consolation,
>   but rather that which is disconsolate;
> Not that which is greatest, but that which is least;
> Not that which is loftiest and most precious,
>   but that which is lowest and most despised;
> Not that which is a desire for anything,
>   but that which is a desire for nothing;
> Strive to go about seeking not the best of temporal
>   things, but the worst;
> Strive thus to desire to enter into complete
> detachment and emptiness and poverty,
> with respect to everything that is in the world.
> For the sake of Jesus Christ, our Lord.
>
> (St John of the Cross, *Ascent of Mount Carmel*, I, 13:6)

You might say "This is beyond our human capacity." True. This is not so much human as it is divine. This is how our Lord operates. He is a great act of self-forgetfulness. We were created to mirror his image. "You are gods" (*Jn* 10:34).

Forgetting about yourself, then, is the core and the crown of prayer. Forgetting about yourself is, in fact, a prayer in itself. It is the exchange of love between the soul and God. In him you forget about yourself. You get ready to give your life as a gift. Forgetting about yourself prepares you for the fifth EVERYTHING, which is the proper relationship with God made entirely of trust. As it is a vast subject, we should analyse it separately.

PART TWO:

TRUST – THE CORRECT RELATIONSHIP WITH GOD

The prayer of faith consists not only in saying "Lord, Lord," but in disposing the heart to do the will of the Father (Mt 7:21).

(*Catechism of the Catholic Church* 2611)

The beauty of silent prayer

Silent prayer leads to the ACT OF FAITH.[2] This is the fifth NOTHING, which is offered to God on the ascent of Mount Carmel. You don't think about yourself but you are open for the will of God to be accomplished in you. You want to sing to the Holy Trinity and make it known to others.

By performing acts of faith, you are allowing God to act in you. There are no barriers to prevent God from acting in you. You are giving everything to him: your mind, your will, your heart, your emotions, your body, your life and your future plans. In return he transforms you into his own tool. An instrument, which is strong and mature. Then you truly find your identity and happiness.

The act of faith is as simple as a child. "I am here. For you. Do whatever you want with me. I love you." You say, "Life to me, of course, is Christ." (*Ph* 1:21) He needs to grow in me and I, myself, should diminish. This is a prayer. The most wonderful prayer.

---

[2] Fr A. Muszala *Silent Prayer*, Catholic Truth Society 2016, p. 26-48

Silent prayer equals the fifth NOTHING whereas prayer in action equals EVERYTHING.

Trust is like a mirror image of the act of faith forming a constant part of your day. You look closer and you see the action of the Holy Spirit in every step you take. You follow his promptings and then you see that whatever you do during your day is not a coincidence but is animated by the presence of God. You don't leave the inner space where you are united with Jesus but you are able, at the same time, to put your heart into all the activities of the day. You are just like Martha of Bethany "beside things but not in things" (Meister Eckhart, *Sermon* 86).

God is present in every event...

The man who abides in the will of God wills nothing else than what God is, and what he wills. If he were ill, he would not wish to be well. If he really abides in God's will, all pain is to him a joy, all complication, simple: yea, even the pains of hell would be a joy to him.

(Meister Eckhart, *Sermon* 4)

God speaks through different events. He confronts us in every way. He offers us opportunities which we should acknowledge and accept. We should co-operate with him to generate a bountiful harvest. Our role is to become like a satellite dish ready to receive the impulses directed towards us. He does not want us to become identified with the following behaviour: "For the heart of this nation has grown coarse, their ears are dull of hearing, and they have shut their eyes, for fear they should see with their eyes, hear with their ears, understand with their heart" (*Mt* 13:15).

God is always surprising us and taking us out of our comfort zone. You see things happen in front of you and you need to react immediately. Do you pick up the coat that has fallen from its hook or pretend you didn't see it? When you see somebody struggling, do you give a hand or not? Do you respond angrily to an offensive statement or not? You need to act quickly in this kind of situation. You need to act "immediately". "Jesus put out his hand at once and held him" (*Mt* 14:31). "Immediately aware that the power had gone out from him, Jesus turned round in the crowed and said, 'Who touched my clothes?'" (*Mk* 5:30).

Spiritual life is very intense. We should be awake and react immediately wherever we are – in the kitchen, at work, in the toilet, in the shopping centre or on the bus. Everything happens for a purpose. God is constantly communicating his will from one event to another. You can pretend you don't hear the Lord or you can respond as Samuel did with the words, "Here I am, since you called me" (*1 S* 3:5) and do what is needed.

God speaks through the various situations and conditions of our lives. God has given you your gender, family, school, university, your job, your country of birth, your home address, all for a purpose. He knows what is best for you and, in God's eyes, where you are is better for you than living under the same roof as John Paul II or Mother Teresa. So you shouldn't think, "If only I was born in a different family; if only I was healthier; if only I had more money…" It is far better to accept the life you have been given and let it become your gift of kindness and love to others. Stop moaning! Stop correcting God's will!

It doesn't mean that you are compelled to do the same job till you retire or that you cannot change your circumstances. In a good relationship with God, you expect to be open to new challenges which enable you to serve better and to love more.

God comes and speaks through joyful events. When you receive a letter or parcel from a loved one, when you hear birdsong in the garden, when you observe the beauty of the stars in the night sky, when you gaze at a beautiful painting or you listen to your favourite piece of music, that is when the Lord is smiling at you, sending you the signs of his kindness. Tell him in the depth of your heart "I love you too". Your prayer can turn into the exclamation of your soul just as Jesus's prayer did: "At that time Jesus exclaimed, 'I bless you, Father, Lord of heaven and of earth, for hiding these things from the learned and the clever and revealing them to mere children'" (*Mt* 11:25).

God also comes through sad and sometimes even dramatic events.

...when we suffer, in sickness and when we die

"Where is he?" This is a common question we ask when we suffer and, especially, when this suffering is caused by the action of others. Where was he when innocent people were suffering in Auschwitz? Where was he when an innocent child died from cancer? There is only one answer to that question and that answer is very difficult to understand. He was and is there with these innocent people as they were dying, because he is the God of sorrow.

> And yet ours were the sufferings he bore,
> Ours the sorrows he carried
> He never opened his mouth
> By the force and by law he was taken
> They gave him a grave with the wicked,
> A tomb with the rich. (*Is* 53:3-9)

God took upon himself all that is human – including sickness, suffering and death – and can say "nothing which is human is alien to me."

God didn't create suffering, but since it came into existence in this world, he uses it to communicate with people. Through sickness he teaches us to be humble and to help one another. He reminds us, silently, that there is no eternal city for us in this life but to look for one in the life to come (*Heb* 13:14). He reminds us that we brought nothing into the world, and we can take nothing out of it (*1 Tm* 6:7). He reminds us that there are far more important things in our life than health and beauty – our spiritual values, to which we should pay more attention. It is he who reminds us to trust him entirely; our trust in him is tested in times of difficulty and not when everything is going well. "For my thoughts are not your thoughts, my ways not your ways – it is the Lord who speaks" (*Is* 55:8).

Sickness, suffering, infertility, miscarriage, death of loved ones, adultery, road accidents, failed exams, bankruptcy, burglary, housefires or flood – these are examples of times of great suffering. It is up to us to trust God in these hard times. "Naked I came from my mother's womb, naked I shall return. The Lord gave, the Lord has taken back. Blessed be the name of the Lord!" (*Jb* 1:21).

Sometimes you rebel; your heart bleeds and you weep. However, if you trust in God, you can utter the most beautiful prayer ever. "Thy will be done." These four words are the essence of the whole of Christian prayer. You need say no more. These four simple words whispered by your soul open the gates of heaven.

Please don't think I glorify sorrow, No! I want to avoid it as much as you do. We do not seek sorrow but, unfortunately, it is an inevitable part of our lives. "From the beginning till now the entire creation, as we know, has been groaning in one great act of giving birth" (*Rm* 8:22). God was there. He is the one who "wipes away all the tears from their eyes; there will be no more death, and no more mourning or sadness. The world of the past has gone" (*Rv* 21:4).

God is really present in everything that happens in our lives despite the fact that we think it goes against his nature. "Jacob said, 'Truly, the Lord is in this place and I never knew it!'" (*Gn* 28:16). This is what we say sometimes too late, too rarely. There is no minute or hour when he is not there. Meister Eckhart once said: "Whatever he did should please us best. Those who do take it as best, ever remain in perfect peace" (Meister Eckhart, *Sermon* 40).

God approaches us in every person we meet

Jeanne Marie was a hermit who lived close to Paris. One day, before going to church for Mass, she was walking among the people in the market square of the big city. She was fascinated with the crowd. She said to her guide, "This is wonderful! I can see Jesus in all these people. Please let me stay longer and walk around him. I have never felt such an intense sense of his presence near me". At once she walked towards a beggar (whom she perceived as Jesus) and stroked his cheek. She didn't speak his language nor did she have anything to offer to him as she was a hermit. The beggar's face shone with a smile. They understood each other. In this one moment heaven witnessed ecstasy, and it was the most beautiful prayer. She showed great love towards him, and he thanked her with his smile. That moment was like a glimpse into eternity despite everybody rushing around minding their own business.

Every person we meet is like an angel sent from God, an angel bearing a message.

When you see a beggar on the street it is as though he is asking, "Will you pass by me without a word?" You don't need to give him any money. Give him an apple, a flower, a brief chat, a smile or, maybe, buy him a sandwich. "For I was hungry and you gave me food; I was thirsty and you gave me drink" (*Mt* 25:35 a-b).

The customer you are serving is Christ himself, who has come to you with a particular request. Look closely and you will find Christ in him. "I was a stranger and you made me welcome" (*Mt* 25:35 c). Make friends with an old, annoying person. This angel in disguise has the mission, by being so irritating, of letting God test your patience. Praise the Lord for sending him and show this person your kindness and love. "I was sick and you visited me; in prison and you came to see me" (*Mt* 25:36 b-c).

The Gospel teaches us to see God in every person. "In so far as you did this to one of the least of these brothers of mine, you did it to me" (*Mt* 25:40).

Act like the good Samaritan who, when he was travelling on the road to Jericho, saw a man who had been beaten and robbed. He felt compassion for the injured man and so he approached him and dressed his wounds. Then he put him on his own donkey and took him to an inn where he looked after him overnight. On leaving the inn the next day, he left money for the man's care but he also left two of the most precious items of currency – hope and love. "Rejoice with those who rejoice and be sad with those in sorrow. Treat everyone with equal kindness (…) let everyone see that you are interested only in the highest ideals" (*Rm* 12:15,17).

We need to seek God in others, and follow the example of those who have done so: in a little baby just as the Three

Wise Men did; in the disabled, like the paralysed man who was healed by Peter as he was walking to the Temple; in the poor, like the freezing beggar with whom Martin of Tours shared his warm cloak; in the unpleasantly sick, like the leper whom Francis of Assisi embraced despite his great horror of leprosy; in the troubled in mind, like the sad and difficult sister of St Thérèse of Lisieux; in the deprived and needy people of the Third World, like those in Africa who were helped by Albert Schweitzer; in those close to death without comfort or solace, like those to whom Mother Teresa gave shelter, comfort and love. This is all called prayer in action. We are put into society so that we can adore the Lord in every person.

We are each a part of the body of Christ, and Jesus is the head. We are composed of different cells which constitute the different parts of the body. Just as cells in our human body are constantly being replaced, we too come and go and are replaced by others. In the same way that blood reaches every cell in our body, the blood of Christ flows into every one of us. One day you will see and understand, with amazement, that every day you were surrounded by Jesus. You will repeat after St Paul: "Since it is in him that we live, and move, and exist" (*Ac* 17:28).

"*Ephphatha*! Wake up". Turn your head from your selfish issues and look up. Look at Zacchaeus who is sitting in the tree, hidden behind leaves of contempt, tears, homelessness, sorrow and pain.

Our wake up call needs to be supported by our resolve as, more often than not, we show an unreasonable fear which paralyses our action. "What will people say?" "Why me?" "I have no time!" We find endless excuses and we shy away and escape the battlefield. This is what happened to the priest and Levite in the Gospel story.

Remember: you are here on earth to do good deeds! Even the smallest act of love saves the world. Because he sees you doing good deeds, God is convinced it is worth keeping the whole of humanity in existence.

One tiny act can save a ladybird from drowning in a puddle; you can save the whole human race from another drowning by forgetting about yourself. This is no exaggeration!

Life in the presence of God

Summing up the previous chapters, we can say that our aim is to live constantly in the presence of God. He comes to us in every single minute. He constantly talks to us.

> Living in the presence of God means allowing prayer to extend and last the whole day, beyond the time we privately allocate for prayer. Prayer isn't just a solitary and distant oasis where we go to seek God during a day full of busy affairs. If prayer were an intellectual exercise, that kind of approach would be acceptable. However, prayer is an act of heart; it involves love and love cannot be confined to a specific time.
>
> (W. Stinissen, *Deep Calls to Deep*)

It goes without saying that we are constantly aware of someone we love. The husband who loves his wife deeply may have to work away from home, yet she is still present in his heart. He knows she will be there waiting for him and they will soon be reunited. His love is reaffirmed deep in his heart when he looks at her photo. His heart is gladdened and he can happily and effectively perform his work.

This is how we should live with God who is our first love. Although nothing can separate us from God's love, it is not at all easy since, unlike the husband who can be physically present with his wife, we are not able to see

God. He seems to be playing a game of hide and seek with us. We have to concentrate to find his presence. How can we do this?

Firstly, start your day by expressing your trust in him, and offering him the whole day. You can do it on the way to work or to your university. Think about what might happen during the day and ask him to give you patience and kindness towards the other people you are going to meet. Ask him to help you to do your work properly and to help you to react positively to all the unexpected events of the day. Then every moment of your day will be transformed into prayer. Do the same with gratitude at the end of your day's work. This doesn't have to take long, only a minute or two. "Every single moment God is communicating himself to us. Most of what occurs in our lives seems to happen accidentally and at random. Now and then God reveals his presence. At times we see the thread and we thank him, but he is always there; everything speaks of him." (W. Stinissen, *Into Your Hands, Father*)

Secondly, lift your heart to the Lord. "Then he took the five loaves and the two fish, raised his eyes to heaven and said the blessing. And breaking the loaves he handed them to his disciples who gave them to the crowds". (*Mt* 14:19)

While you are occupied with some task, you can briefly turn towards the Lord and repeat your act of faith saying, "I am yours", "My God and my only God" or something similar. It only needs to be a very short prayer such as one you said in the Act of Faith during your morning prayer. The thing is to remember to do it and not to lose yourself entirely in the work in hand. You can use reminders like the alarm on your mobile phone, switching your wristwatch on to the other hand, hearing an ambulance alarm or your midday coffee break. Whenever you are forced to wait for someone or something, instead of feeling impatient, why not make it an opportunity to be with God? There are many ways to avoid losing yourself in your tasks.

"A mere uplifting of the heart is enough. A thought about God, inner adoration even in a rush – they are the prayers, which please God although they are short" (Brother Lawrence of the Resurrection, *The Practice of the Presence of God*).

Do as Jesus did, constantly standing near his Father. "Then Jesus lifted his eyes and said: 'Father I thank you for hearing my prayer. I know indeed that you always hear me'" (*Jn* 11:41-42).

Thirdly, try to stay focused and control your thoughts. Don't let them wander about. Restrain your imagination and discipline your thinking. If you don't do that, your silent prayer will be more difficult. "Every time we realise we are fantasising we need to turn and rebuild our relationship with God immediately. Not only when we pray but when we eat, wash ourselves, when we walk or wait for the bus or when we wake up at night" (W. Stinissen, *Deep Calls to Deep*).

Fourthly, remember everything is in God's hands and God is looking after us. In fact, there are no coincidences. No person is put in our path without God's plan. He looks at us with love and kindness. You are on the Holy Spirit's radar. "He plants in us a single desire: to keep our eyes on the Master, to whom we have given ourselves and to be constantly on the alert to divine his will and execute it immediately" (J.P. de Caussade, *Abandonment to Divine Providence*).

Fifthly, be open to all new challenges and opportunities. Do not tie yourself to any place on earth or to people like some do. Be flexible, just like clay in God's hands, so he can mould you to whatever form he wishes.

Living up to the above suggestions will make you an implement in God's hands. All events, meetings, work, relaxations, will be directed by God. All is planned. Your Guide is next to you. You are like a child led by the Holy Spirit. God is your rock. You will be able to rely on everything happening calmly and peacefully. You have given everything to him and now you can live your life freely.[3]

---

[3] J. P. de Caussade, *Abandonment to Divine Providence*

Living every minute

The present moment, then, is like a desert in which the soul sees only God whom it enjoys; and is only occupied with those things which he requires of it, leaving and forgetting all else, and abandoning it to Providence.

(J.P. de Caussade, *Abandonment to Divine Providence*)

Synonymous with living in the presence of God is living every moment to the full. You do not absent yourself by looking into the future or looking back to the past. You realise it is this moment NOW when you need to give a hundred per cent of yourself. This NOW lasts only a second and contains God's will at that very instant.

A young man whom Jesus urged to sell his possessions and follow him had only a second to decide what to do. He failed, and was not offered a second chance.

The tax collector, Matthew, was given a similar amount of time to decide. He looked at the money, got up and followed Jesus.

It takes a mere fraction of a second for a person to stumble down a staircase in front of you. An immediate reaction to help can possibly prevent a more severe fall leading to broken bones and a long and painful recovery.

How quickly do you recognise the needs and offer help to those whom you pass by each day? People often need your help immediately, like the blind person trying to cross a busy road or the stranger, lost and bewildered, at the railway station. Terminally ill patients in the hospice cannot wait until tomorrow!

> In the first ages souls were more simple and straightforward. Then, for those who led a spiritual life, each moment brought some duty to be faithfully accomplished. Their whole attention was thus concentrated consecutively like a hand that marks the hours which, at each moment, traverses the space allotted to it. (J.P. de Caussade, *Abandonment to Divine Providence*)

Perhaps we should say more about the "sacrament of the present moment"?

A sacrament it is a visible sign of the invisible presence of God. This presence is visible in every moment of our life. For example, this very moment when you read this book: God is saying something to you. He is teaching you something. In a few moments the "sacrament of the present moment" will become a phone conversation with a very annoying person. Maybe it will be hunger and sleepiness that have to be conquered within the rhythm of daily tasks or the workload of the priesthood. Don't postpone things until tomorrow. If you have to complete a task that you do not relish, do it first. If you are expecting a difficult conversation, don't put it off. If you have a project with a deadline at the end of the month, complete it a week early. God prefers you to do this rather than spending great amounts of time in church or choosing to do something that you would prefer for yourself. Living the "sacrament of the present moment" will cost you more.

Age quod agis, "Whatever you do, do it well." says St Ignatius Loyola. In other words, "Don't do ten things at once, but concentrate on the task given to you by God, now, at this very moment." Do it properly.

> Perhaps the secret can be found in certain saints who died young and who came an incredibly long way in their short time. Not a moment of their life was lost. Nothing that happened was in vain. They knew that, at every moment, in every event and circumstance, not least in that which seemed to destroy their "spiritual life", God gave them a little nudge in the back, and they let themselves be pushed by him. (W. Stinissen, *Into Your Hands, Father*)

Spiritual life is extremely dynamic, intensive and fast. It is just like running a marathon (St Paul). It is all about concentration; staying alert, so that we do not miss something important. It is all about being conscious of the fact that the time given to us, to suffer and die to ourselves, is a one-off opportunity. Therefore we must not miss this unique chance. "Living in the present is actually an invaluable exercise. We work and cease to work, we read and put the book down again, we speak and are silent, eat and sleep; always totally present, but in a constantly changing environment" (W. Stinissen, *Into Your Hands, Father*).

Hodie. Only today counts. This moment deepens you into eternity. Deepens you in endlessness.

Constant prayer

Stay awake, praying at all times
(*Lk* 21:36)

The Eastern Church developed the practice of constant prayer, commonly called, "The Jesus Prayer". The essence of this prayer is to repeat, "God be merciful to me, a sinner" (*Lk* 18:14) many times. The power of this prayer lies in calling upon the name of God as often as a thousand times a day. St Paul writes: "so all the beings in the heavens, on earth and in the underworld, should bend the knee at the name of Jesus" (*Ph* 2:10). The more often one calls upon the name of God, the more one is united with him and is able to withstand all evil. According to the teaching of the *Philokalia*, the name of Jesus, revealed by the angel at the Annunciation, has the power of God's presence. By calling on the name of Jesus, the presence of God is infused into the soul.

The Western Church focused on a different aspect of spiritual life. Thanks to St Thomas Aquinas, St John of the Cross and St Thérèse of the Child Jesus, another model of inner prayer was developed. Inner prayer leads to entire trust in God. Such a prayer, silent prayer, should be practised once a day.

But what would happen if we attempted to amalgamate Eastern and Western models of prayer? In today's world of advanced technology, constant rush and complex issues, it would prove impossible to adopt the Jesus Prayer as the Egyptian hermits, the monks of Mount Athos or the Elders (*startsy*) of the Optina Monastery in Russia did. But that need not prevent us from making many acts of faith throughout the day and, in each daily event, recognising the action of the Holy Spirit. Far from leading to a deep anxiety derived from the tension between our inner self and our worldly self, this would enable us to experience unity with God, with our fellow human beings and with the whole of creation.

Each meeting with other people would be a meeting with Jesus. Each conversation would be a prayer. The work we do would be fulfilling God's will. Each joyful event would be praising the Holy Trinity. Each sorrow would be a chance to forget about ourselves. Each suffering would be treated as an invitation to deeper unity with God. Each temptation would be a spiritual battle in the name of God. Each meal would be a supper with God. Each holiday would be an introduction to Heaven. This is the essence of constant prayer.

Constant prayer is like a heart which is constantly awake. It requires being alive to every moment, ready to respond to Jesus as he comes to meet us in each event of the day. Without a word being spoken, we address him through the actions we perform in our daily routine. This is how we accomplish his mission. Not once, but again. And again. And yet again…

The Jesus Prayer and the act of faith are two compatible paths leading to unity with God. They complement each other, just like the Eastern and Western traditions. They are like twin lungs that provide "oxygen" to energise theology and spirituality. This is a kind of ecumenical prayer. It enables the two churches to be joined as one.

This is the type of prayer that St Thérèse of the Child Jesus discovered and practised. One day she confided to her sister Céline that there were not even three minutes in the day when she would not be thinking about God. She dedicated her life to being constantly alert, responding with an act of faith for each call from heaven, even during the time when she was suffering the dark night of the soul.

"Although I have no joy of faith, I still try to carry out the works of faith. This last year, I believe I have made more acts of faith than during the rest of my life" (St Thérèse of Lisieux, *Manuscript C*, 7r).

Thérèse the little flower of Lisieux was always alert, always ready to run after the one she gave her heart to. Always present. She always chose EVERYTHING. She always focused on acting lovingly, even towards an extremely annoying elderly sister and the harsh novice mistress.

We started this book with St Thérèse of the Child Jesus and we will finish with her. We ask her to pray for us to make a "marathon" of our life as she did.

> My life is only this moment,
> An hour which is just passing
> My life is like a day which is passing and running away
> You God know about this
> That I can love you here
> Only this day, this single day.
> (St Thérèse of Lisieux, *Poems*, 5)

The end

Regarding prayer, we can begin to understand that it is not just saying words, or a special time devoted to Jesus.

Prayer is a new lifestyle. Prayer, as the ancient theologian says, is *elevatio mentis ad Deum*[4], lifting our spirit to God where God beholds Jesus and by this means he beholds you and me.

Prayer is like staying online with the one who loved us first. If you live in this way, God listens to your every prayer. You are "directing God's will" (St Teresa of Avila) as your prayers are never selfish. Your prayer is listened to by God before you even articulate it. Over the years, you eventually become a walking prayer. Just like Jesus. And his Mother. Fiat!

---

[4] John of Damascus, *On the Faith*, III, 24